The Little Book of Iron Age Skills

by Will Llawerch

Foreword

There are so many books regarding the Celts and the Celtic world on the market today that it can be difficult to discover anything more about the Iron Age people than they were warriors who painted themselves blue and their priesthood were called druids.

Since it is original publication in 2007, there have been several extraordinarily important archaeological finds which have increased our knowledge about the Iron Age Britons & Celts significantly. However, researching the contents of this book I made the conscious decision to focus attentions away from the world of warriors and their religious beliefs.

Instead, this little book has been designed to help you imagine some of the most mundane but necessary everyday life skills used by people in the Iron Age.

Will Llawerch 2019 ©

Table of Contents

Should We Call them Celts or Britons?

The Iron Age people referred to in this book are Britons and Gauls. The Gauls were the inhabitants of what is now modern France who in turn belonged to a group of people stretching across Europe which shared many similar religious, cultural & linguistic connections but who at a tribal level looked vastly different from one another. In the more recent Past, archaeologists have preferred to draw all these tribes together for ease of labelling, referring to them as 'The Celts'.

This term, 'The Celts' has been misleading, and many people today think that the inhabitants of Britain and Ireland were also Celts. However, it is now generally accepted that the Britons and Gauls were different cultural groups but whom both understood iron production and traded with one another.

When the Roman's spoke of the Gaul's, Gallia or Celtae they were referring to different tribes of people who stretched from the North of Italy to France, from southern Germany to parts of Spain.

We know that the basis for their language was shared but had many regional dialects, they worshipped the same God's and Goddesses, but each tribe used variations on the names of these deities.

Britons and those Iron Age people in Ireland are accepted to have been descendants of the Bronze Age farmers and earlier who had lived in Britain and Ireland since the Stone Age or before the water levels rose and separated them from the European continent. The Romans tell us that they too considered the Britons to be separate from Gauls, however; Caesar describes trade between the south east of Britain and the Gauls and notes that in those areas the communities were remarkably similar.

So, for the purposes of this book, by Iron Age people I mean both Britons and Gauls whom were both extraordinarily successful and imaginative in their production and use of Iron.

What did the Iron Age People Look like?

Fig. 1 (left) and 2 (right)

The Classical writers both Roman and Greek describe the Gauls as tall, fair skinned with well-developed muscles. Their stories and saga's dating back to the late Bronze Age, such as "The Ulster Cycle" & The Mabinogion, describe both the ideal warrior and woman. Warriors strove to keep themselves in good physical condition and preferred to have blonde hair, even dyeing their hair if it was not already so. Women are described as being of equal stature to their men and the most beautiful had swan white skin and long hair.

But archaeology gives us another picture. After studying skeletons from many Iron Age sites in Britain and Europe, archaeologists can get a better, more accurate picture of what the general population of Gauls and Britons were really like.

There is a general belief that people in the olden days were shorter than us, however that is not true. New research suggests that since before the early bronze age, the average height for men has been about 5ft 7inches (170cms) and for women, 5ft 3inches(160cm) They were no doubt a lot fitter than us because of our ever more sedentary lifestyles in the 21st century.

The evidence from Bog Bodies, with their neatly trimmed fingernails and well-kept beards and hair proves that the Iron Age people liked to look after their appearance. One recent discover in Ireland show's us the use of pine resin to ac as a hair gel.

I think the two factors which differ the most between us in the 21st century and the Iron Age people of 2000 years ago are firstly physical anomalies, growth defects due to disease and injury. These were probably more evident amongst the smaller populations and probably more accepted. Secondly, average life expectancy was generally shorter for both men and women but for different reasons.

Besides illness, famine and disease, women generally had a greater chance of death between the ages 14-20 during childbirth. Men it seems had a significant chance of dying in warfare.

What did Iron Age People Eat?

Fig.3

Some movies and cartoons show the Celts eating big joints of wild boar around blazing campfires every night. But it is important to remember that neither ancient Greek Olympic athletes nor Roman Gladiators ever ate red meat. In fact, Gladiators were some of the fittest individuals at this time in history and they were nicknamed 'Barley-eaters"

In my opinion, even in an Iron Age community such feasting would have happened only on special occasions and the Iron Age people probably ate some of the following food on a day to day basis instead:

- *Vegetable soups with leeks, onions, wild garlic, turnips, parsnips, and cabbage.*
- *Wild nuts like hazelnuts, Berries like gooseberries, blackberries, elderberries & blueberries.*
- *Porridge made from rolled oats*
- *Flat breads,*
- *Eggs from their hens and wild bird's eggs*
- *Honey from local bees*
- *Chicken and Fish like trout, mackerel, and salmon*

- *Seaweed, crabs, mussels, mollusks*
- *Nettles, Fennel, Common Sorrel, Wild Garlic, Parsley, Spinach*
- *Wild Mushrooms****
- *Wild animals like Bear, fox, beaver, deer, wild boar, ducks, wild birds, frogs etc.*
- *Black puddings & Sausages*
- *Some domesticated animals like goats, sheep, and pigs.*

**** If you cannot identify which wild mushrooms are poisonous, do not eat any of them*

What did Iron Age People Drink?

The Gauls & Britons would not have known what coffee or fizzy drinks are, and no doubt they were better off for it. But what choice did they have when they were thirsty?

Milk & Water

Undoubtedly milk from goats and cattle was a staple drink amongst both children and adults with water from a natural spring also being available in plentiful supply. However, we must ask what percentage of their population did bother to drink fresh water from springs?

Herbal Tea

They certainly did not have black tea as we know it, but they must have found comfort in a bowl of herbal tea. By adding different herbs to hot water various minor ailments could be relieved. For instance, living close to the smoke from an open fire daily, Sage could be given to ease asthma and pleurisy; wild mint would be given to settle an upset stomach, chamomile to help relax the whole body. They would have sweetened all the above by simply adding honey.

Alcohol

Even in ancient times alcohol was particularly important, especially amongst the Iron Age people who were noted by the Romans for drinking vast quantities of it as part of their many social activities. Ancient writers tell us that the poorer folk drank a form of wheat beer and that strong mead (from honey) was fermented also. However, the higher up the social ladder you were, it seems you would more than likely want to be seen to drink red wine.

Red wine would have had to have been imported from the Mediterranean and by drinking red wine you were showing your neighbours that you could afford to do so. The Roman's make a point of reference that the Celts drank the wine neat, instead of diluting it a little as was the Roman custom.

What did the Iron Age People Wear?

When you compare the few original remains of Iron Age clothing in the form of trousers and long-sleeved, thigh length tunics, with much later Dark Age varieties, there is at a practical level very little difference. The original design being so adept at keeping people warm and dry, comfortable and without a need for constant repair.

Shoes

Unlike modern shoes, Iron Age shoes did not have raised heels and were not made to last. In fact, most people would probably have worn a form of 'turn shoe'. Similar shoes were still in use in parts of Scotland and Ireland until the early 20th Century. People by the coast we know used seal skin and soaked their shoes in a pail of saltwater over night to keep them soft.

Fig. 4

In Scotland, turn shoes were made from one piece of leather cut to cover the foot with a tongue and flaps. The only stitching required was at the back to form a closed heel. There were of course many different styles of Iron Age shoe, some intricately decorated sandals, others resembling soft slippers. Whatever the style it is certain that such shoes were probably only worn for one season and then thrown away and new ones made. It is important to remember that the tanning techniques used for leather in the Iron Age produced only brown colours. (See shoe patterns in end notes)

Trousers

The Romans and Greeks tell us that the Gauls and Britons were well known for wearing trousers which they called 'Braccae'. As we know the Iron Age people were great horsemen and in the cooler climates of north Western Europe and Britain trousers make sense. Wearing trousers on horseback is practical and in fact the Roman cavalry wore leather knee length breeches.

Although Braccae were obviously quite common to the Iron Age people, archaeologists have only found one pair of intact trousers from a peat bog in Angeln, modern day Denmark. So, we must look at the few sculptures which the Romans made of the Celts and, we must look at the Celtic coins which depict warriors wearing full length trousers. If making your own Iron Age costume, drawstring waists and belt loops are acceptable. Trousers gathered with leather drawstrings at the ankles are personal choice.

Fig. 5
An Iron Age Woman in Peplos Wool Dress and Cloak.

Dresses, Skirts

We do not know whether women wore trousers the same as the men sometimes. Generally, archaeologists portray women in the Iron Age wearing a small variety of dresses.

One is the basic, 'A' shaped dress with or without long sleeves which is stitched along each edge. Another style is to wear a waist length tunic (with or without sleeves) with an over dress stitched ¾ of the way up the sides, or up to just below your arm and leave everything above it open. Pull it over the top of the tunic and hold the two top edges together at each shoulder with brooches. All dresses should be worn down to the ankles and drawn in around the waist with a belt.

The dresses should not be too close fitting, however there is a theory that the nobility would have been able to afford to have material cut and so their clothes and dresses may have been tailored to a greater extent.

Cloaks

The Romans describe the Gauls of Europe wearing short, light wool summer cloaks. In Ireland bodies have been found accompanied by thick heavy wool cloaks sometimes lined with softer, lighter wool. The cloaks found preserved in peat bogs show at least a couple of different patterns of cloak. It is difficult to say whether there was a definite 'Celtic' style cloak, but it is worth noting that the Romans seem to have preferred to use wool with high lanolin content (natural oil from sheep's wool). A design which Roman writers suggest is a Gaulish cloak.

The lanolin would make the cloak waterproof and less liable to be saturated with water and become heavy and uncomfortable. Whichever style you wish to recreate, be advised to buy the largest 100% wool blanket you can find. The minimum practical size will be at least 65 inches x 60 inches.

Pouches

We do not know whether men and women had trouser pockets in the Iron Age, so most re-enactors and Celtic enthusiasts wear simple leather drawstring pouches on their belts. Others might wear leather shoulder bags with fringes. Perhaps children whose job it was to keep birds away from the crops wore large leather bags full of sling stones.

Jewelry

Both the Romans and Greeks tell us that the Celts were well known for their love of Gold and Silver jewelry. But the enthusiasts who spend time living like the Iron Age people have discovered that if you try to wear the same styles of jewelry as ancient authors describe, many of the daily tasks carried out in the Iron Age mean that the bangles and neck torcs and rings more often than not simply get in the way and are impractical. This perhaps tells us that only the wealthy people wore jewelry because they did not have to work.

Both penannular and fibula brooches were worn by both men and women in the Iron Age. Penannular brooches can be made from silver and bronze, but many would have been iron. The fibula brooches generally are bronze sometimes silver inlaid with coral studs and very ornate.

Ladies of wealth certainly possessed elaborate bronze hand mirrors and wooden or bone hair combs. We also know that women in the Iron Age may well have used make up and pigments would have been created from wild berries. Their hair seems to have been worn long and was more often than not braided or plaited elaborately. Though it is accepted that people generally wore their hair longer than we do today, I believe that the professional warriors would have had shorter hair. It is less of a liability in battle and when lime washed it does resemble boar's hackles as the Classical writers describe.

Tunics

The Iron Age men wore a style of top called a tunic. Do not confuse this with the Roman soldiers 'Tunica'. The Tunic would have been made from wool and measure down to the mid-thigh. It is generally accepted that these tunics would have had a simple oval shaped head hole. It could be sleeveless or with full length sleeves. The statue from Vacheres, France thought to represent a Gaulish nobleman even shows turn-back-cuffs and scalloping.

Another form of tunic may have been the same as above but with an open front. Such a wraparound tunic may have been held closed by a belt or even wooden toggles.

The Classical writers tell us that the Celtic people loved to wear brightly coloured clothes of complicated checkered patterns, stripes, and plaids such as tabby weave and hound's tooth. This does not mean that the Iron Age people wore modern tartans. But certainly, you would expect to see reds, blues, greens, yellows and a whole variety of browns and earth tones.

The lower status you were in Iron Age society, such as slaves captured in battle, the fewer colours and less complicated the patterns you could probably afford to wear.

We know that during their dyeing processes, the Iron Age people only seem to have had salt as a fixer for the colours and so one would expect to see once bright colours fade within a year.

Fig. 6

Underwear

There is unfortunately no evidence for wearing underwear; however modern enthusiasts who recreate the clothing have discovered that if you are wearing wool next to the skin on hot days, as the body sweats the wool clogs the pores in the skin and encourages itchiness, rashes and even fungal infections. It is perfectly reasonable for Britons and Gauls to have worn linen under shirts, under dresses and maybe even knee length under trousers. However, although there is evidence from the Roman fort at Vindolanda on Hadrian's wall that at least one soldier asked for socks and underwear to be sent, there is absolutely no evidence for knitted socks or loincloth style underwear at all amongst the Britons and Gauls.

The Ice Man who was discovered in the Alps in 1991 dates from 2,300 years before the Iron Age and his shoes were stuffed with long grass to insulate his feet in winter. Until we find evidence of Gaulish socks, then enthusiasts will have to have either cold feet with no insulation or warm feet with the same long grasses in their shoes.

Belts

Belts are useful and some might say essential for hanging things like pouches and daggers. Use leather, straight or plaited. The belt will fasten at the front with a belt hook. Belt buckles from the Iron Age period are very distinctive. The Iron Age people used what we call belt hooks. These are a simple iron, or bronze ring with a hook on the outside edge. You might also expect to see belt hooks carved from a piece of bone however, these are brittle and do not last long with heavy usage.

Another style of belt requires no buckles and is cut down the centre at one end making two long laces like strips. On the other end of the belt a hole is punched and when placed around the waist the long strips go through the hole and then tie over and under the belt to keep it from coming undone easily.

In its simplest form, a belt could have a hole punched at one and a carved wooden toggle sewn to the other end. The toggle passes through the hole to fasten.

Linen Production

Remember, most of the clothing and cloaks was undoubtedly wool of differing thickness. However, I am sure that neither the Britons nor Gauls ever walked around in the heat of the summer months all wrapped up in wool. If you are looking for a lighter material for tunics or ladies' outer dresses for the summer months, then pure linen is ideal.

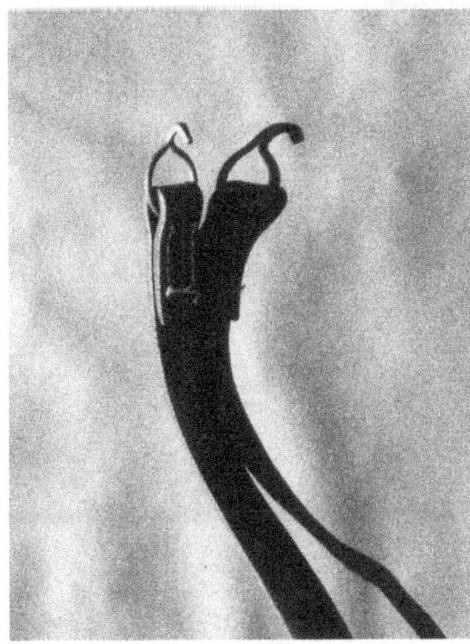

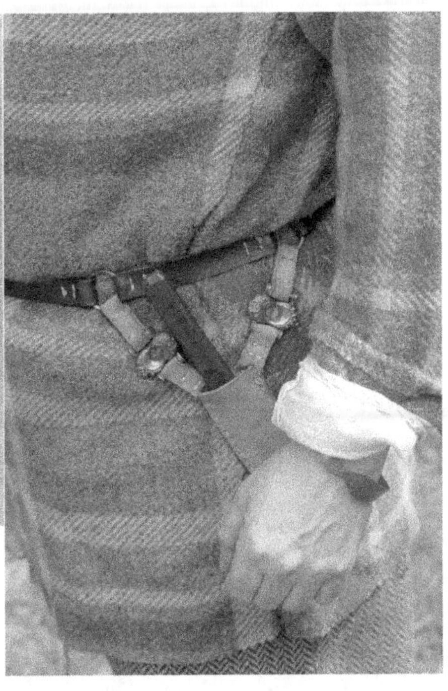

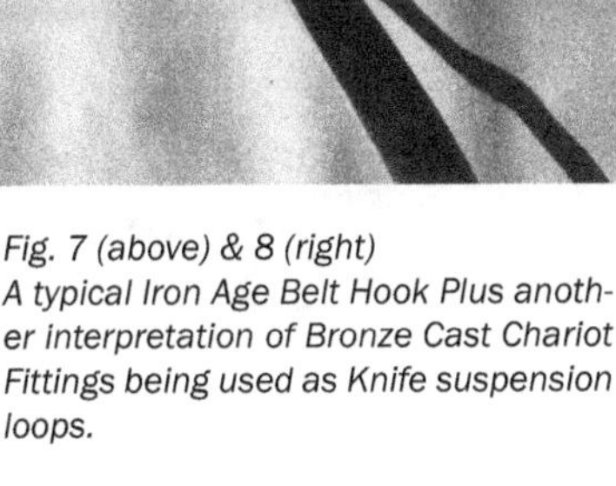

Fig. 7 (above) & 8 (right)
A typical Iron Age Belt Hook Plus another interpretation of Bronze Cast Chariot Fittings being used as Knife suspension loops.

Linen thread has been known since at least the Bronze Age and is made from the inner strands of the flax stalk. By the Iron Age, Flax was a crop, planted and harvested like Emmer wheat and barley. However, the flax was probably rarely eaten. Instead the inner strands were used in linen production and the flax seeds were used to produce oil.

After harvesting, the Britons and Gauls allowed the long flax stalks to 'ret' or degrade in water for about a week, the outer stalks are then crushed with a wooden mallet. Inside the crushed stalk a thin white core is exposed and is then removed. Once collected the white inner strands are combed repeatedly to remove dirt and small debris left by the crushed stalks. Once cleaned, the gathered flax looks a little like candy floss. This is then ready to be spun into a fine thread using Iron Age drop spindles.

Fig. 9

1/ Remove the seeds with a coarse toothed hatchel

Fig. 10

2/ Allow the Flax to Ret

Fig. 11
3/ removed from stalk and cleaned

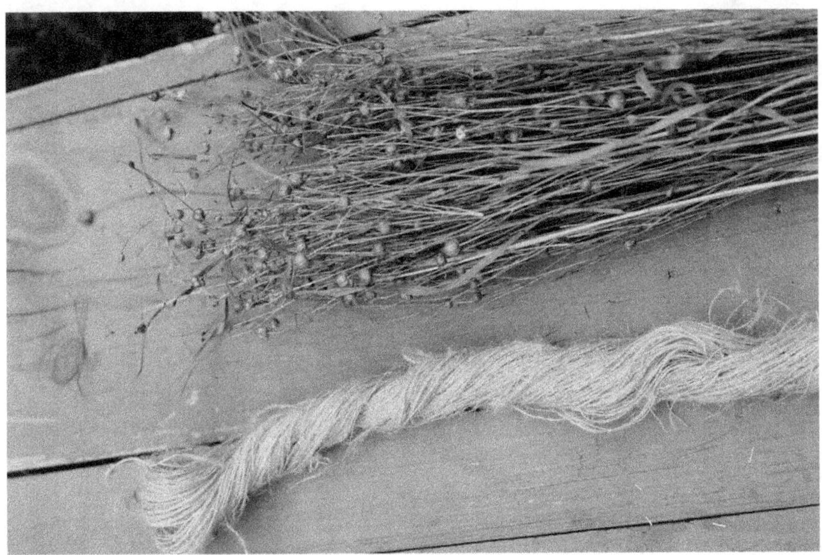

Fig. 12
4/ A skein of spun flax and the plant it came from

The drop spindle would have been a common daily activity and may have taken place solely during the summer months with weaving taking place during the long dark winter months because it is more important to 'feel' what you are weaving rather than see what you are weaving and on the other hand its more important to see the thread you are spinning to ensure its even.

Interestingly enough, before dyeing, fresh woven linen resembles a light fawn brown colour and only becomes pure white through repeated wearing and washing. So, the notion of a clean sparkling white shirt was purely a 20th century ideal.

Below, you will see a reconstruction of an Iron Age Linen shirt with embroidered icons taken from Iron age coins.

Fig. 13

Sheep to Shawl

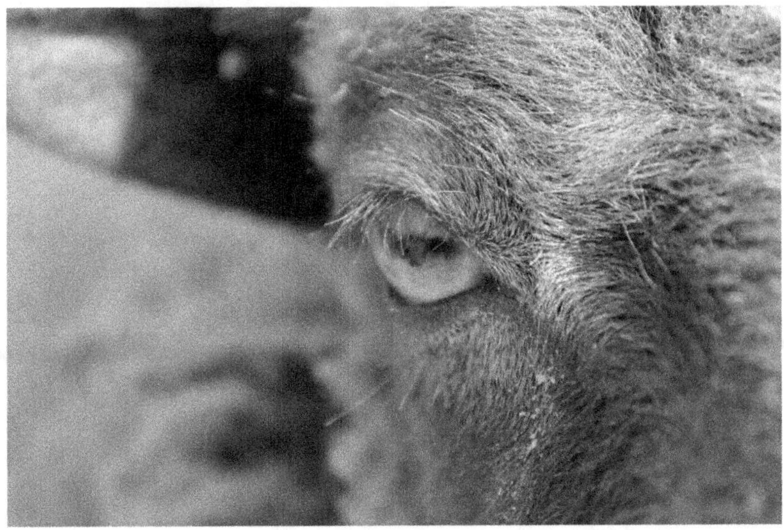

Fig. 14

In this chapter, we will be looking at how you take the wool from a sheep and turn it into something we can wear.

Fig. 15
Unprocessed sheep's fleece.

Fig. 16 (above)
Washed, cleaned, and waiting to be carded.

Fig. 17 (left)
A Warp Weighted loom.

Ancient breeds of sheep in the Iron Age were similar to horned Soay Sheep and generally brown in colour. Unlike their modern variety, ancient sheep do not need shearing; instead, their wool coat is plucked by hand.

Once the wool is collected it would be washed two or three times in hot soapy water. Then, once clean enough to handle, the wool is carded to break down the fibres and to remove any grass or twigs.

The next step is to create a thread which can be woven from the carded fibres using a drop spindle.

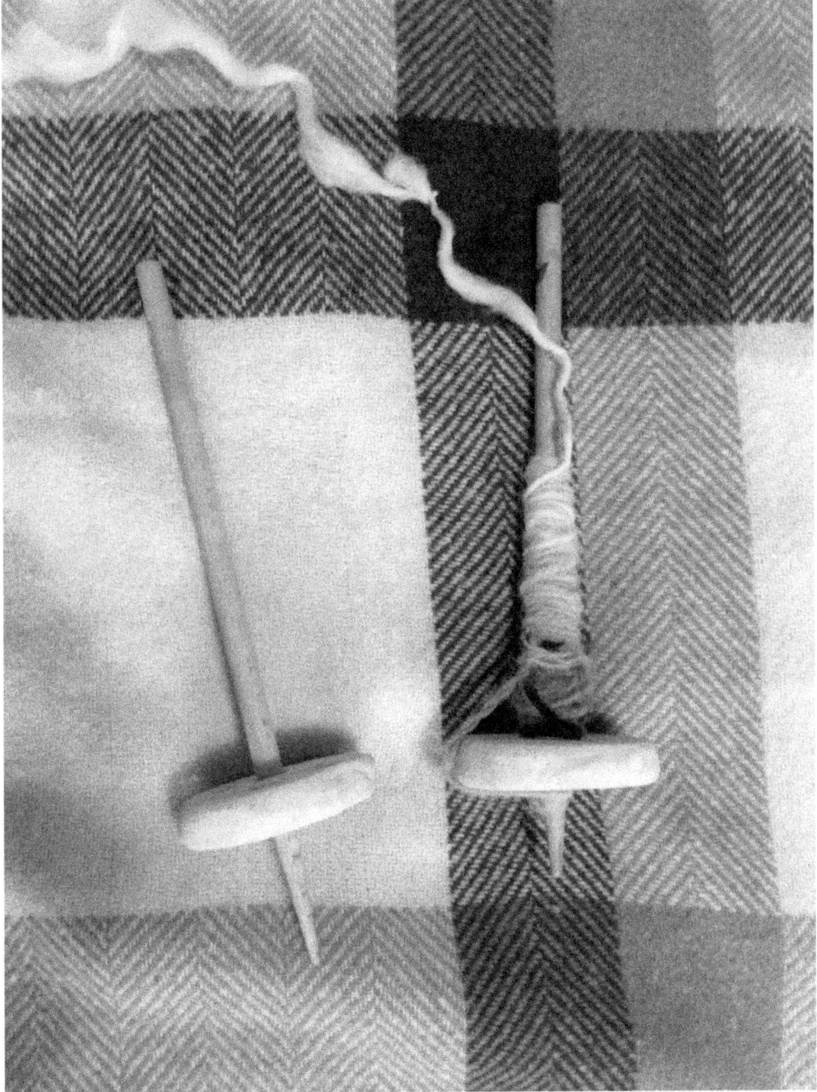

Fig. 18
Two Reproduction Iron Age Drop Spindles on a piece of loom woven cloth.

Finally, once spun, the threads can be woven into cloth using a warp weighted loom for clothes and trade. Spun on a drop spindle to create wool for weaving.

Fig. 19
Warp weighted loom.

The Iron Age Roundhouse

Fig. 20

No matter what the Romans may have thought, we know that the ancient Iron Age people were the same as 21st century humans; they were as inventive and creative as us and no doubt sometimes as lazy as us. However, it is also true that no matter how much we would like to try, a 21st century person with their modern thoughts and ideas can never totally immerse themselves in the original mindset of the ancients. Archaeology hints at the interiors of houses being divided up into areas of different activity. For example, Weaving on a loom near the entrance, perhaps storage at the back with bedroom on the right. Roman writers suggest to us that there would have been a day-time side and a night-time side mentality to how the house was viewed and used.

But when people volunteer to live for extended stays in reconstructed Celtic villages and do more than wear the clothes and eat the food, as archaeologists, we can if we are lucky get the briefest glimpse into what life might have been like in the ancient world.

So how should we imagine a round house and the kind of necessary work that went on within it each day?

Instead of carrying pails of water back and forth as needed on an hourly basis, the largest cauldron in the house was placed close to or above the fire in the hearth to ensure a constant supply of hot water.

All the cooking pots would have had wooden lids to stop the ash from the fire falling into them.

The iron pots at the end of each day would have been washed, dried, and then coated inside with fat to keep the rust out. Then each morning, the pots were washed again, the fat removed, and food cooked.

During the winter, vegetables and fruit were not readily available, but in the autumn time, the Iron Age people would have strung vegetable and fruit slices up to dry in their granaries or even in their houses. In the winter, the dried foods could be placed in boiling water and reconstituted to form soups or pie fillings.

The earth floors of the houses were leveled perfectly with a mixture of clay, dung, and straw. This made it easy to sweep them clean and in some cases their houses even had floorboards.

Fig. 21

The Romans tell us that the Britons and Gauls sat on sheepskins strewn on the floor. However, we know they had framed wooden beds. Therefore, even if they had no chairs, we could expect to see low tables for food preparation by the fireplace.

How many people lived in a roundhouse?

We do not really know if all the gossiping old women lived in one house or if all the warriors lived together in the largest house. But we can guess that many generations of families probably lived together. So, you can imagine living with your mum and dad, your brothers and sisters, your grandparents and perhaps even an aunt or uncle and their spouses.

Fig. 22

There was probably extraordinarily little privacy, but this helped keep the whole community close and able to support one another. Archaeologists believe that in a typical round house there would be separate walled off rooms for beds with small storage areas between them. Perhaps the bed stalls as we call them may even have had thick, colourful woven curtains which could be closed at night.

However, the Iron Age people, being largely an agricultural society probably spent little time in their houses during the day. They were an out-doors people and so maybe only mothers; infants and old people could be expected to be in the house during the day.

Fig. 23

Fig. 24
Hot embers from the central hearth with the open doors behind.

An Iron Age Child's Day

It is important to remember that in the Iron Age, unless you were born into a noble or rich family, your life was mostly hard physical toil. Your working life revolved around keeping your chieftain in the position to which he or she was accustomed.

Waking up at first light and going to bed just after last light, the natural rhythm of the day and seasons would have controlled the kind of work you had to do each day. There was no such thing as health and safety and no time for children to simply do whatever they wanted. Children were almost certainly given jobs of responsibility from an early age.

Many of the jobs were taken for granted, but without them the community and life in the Iron Age would have been difficult.

- Fetching water, perhaps a few the older children would have carried pails of water from the natural spring in or around the community each morning.
- Milking goats and tending livestock, using sling stones to keep foxes and other predators away. Grinding corn with quern stones to make their families bread each day.
- Clearing birds and pests from crops at planting time with sling stones.
- Cleaning sheep's wool and preparing it or spinning on drop spindles.
- Making soap from lye (ash from the fire) and lanolin (from sheep's wool)
- Operating bellows for the blacksmith at the bloom furnace and in his forge.

How They Made Fire

Fig. 25

Throughout history, fire was perhaps the most important element for the benefit of day to day living and teaching children how to make fire was perhaps one of the first things they learnt.

Tinder can be made from wild mushroom, the bracket fungus which grows on trees are excellent, also some dried grasses, twigs, birch bark and wood from the forest known as 'old man's beard'.

Strike the flint against the iron with a downward motion. Some people like to hold a piece of the mushroom against the iron with their thumb to catch the spark and they hold the flint in their other hand. I prefer to place the crumbled mushroom in a shallow bowl with a flat bottom. Whichever way you prefer, it can take a bit of practice, but the old saying 'practice makes perfect' means that within a few hours of doing it regularly a good hot ember is achievable within a minute or two.

- Once the sparks have caught the mushroom and become an ember stop striking and start blowing gently adding small amounts of tinder.
- Once you have a good hot ember, tip it out of the bowl into the dried grass and fold the grass over it.

- Next waft the grass back and forth at arm's length to get oxygen to the ember. You should see smoke start to appear.
- Once the grass starts to smoke heavily and fire appears, tip the whole thing into the hearth where your pre prepared sticks of 'Old man's beard' wood sit.
- Both old man's beard and Elm are particularly good wood for this because they burn hot, quickly and with hardly any smoke.

Fig. 26

Iron Production

1/ Charcoal Burning

Charcoal undoubtedly was a significant part of the Iron Age. Without it, neither iron, bronze, copper, or tin would have been produced, the clean hot embers were used for cooking on the central hearths of roundhouses and would not have been large log fires billowing smoke everywhere. The art of Charcoal burning was essential to the whole society. Gangs of charcoal burners would have been continually producing charcoal year-round.

Charcoal is created by burning wood slowly over 24 hours as part of a controlled burn. The Iron Age people would have used only certain kinds of wood to make charcoal with; Ash, Oak and Horse chestnut were commonly used. The wood was cut into small logs of uniform size and left to season for up to 9 months before being stacked into a cone shape making sure that in the centre a clear area was left.

When the kiln is full a fire is lit in the central clear area. Once the fire has caught most of the wood, then the top of the kiln can be covered with turf to limit the amount of oxygen. This controlled burn should continue for 24hrs and this is the most dangerous part due to some of the more volatile chemical reactions taking place inside. Charcoal burners would have to sit up awake all night to watch carefully. If the kiln failed it could become a highly fueled raging inferno and set fire to all the forest around. Once the burning process is complete, the kiln is then allowed to cool down over a few days before the turf can be removed and the charcoal placed in baskets ready to be carried to the industries that needed them.

Fig. 27
Cut logs ready to stack.

Fig. 28
Stacked logs ready for covering with earth.

Fig. 29
Charcoal kiln ready to be lit.

Fig. 30
Operating the bellows of the bloom furnace.

As you can imagine, with so much timber being required, even a small community would outstrip its supply of wood within a generation making permanent settlements impossible. However, we know the Iron Age people built some huge, permanent settlements across Britain and Europe. Archaeology provides us with evidence that even the earlier Bronze Age communities understood woodland management and how important coppicing and replanting trees was.

Where does Iron come from?

Fig. 31

Iron is an ore. The ore is a red coloured rock and in certain parts of Britain the seam of iron ore was visible above ground and samples of ore could be simply picked up off the ground and placed in baskets ready for transporting to the Bloom furnaces for smelting. If you look carefully at a piece of iron ore, you can see the iron content with the naked eye as a grey streak running through the red rock. You can also tell which rock has the iron in it simply by its weight.

However, just because you have filled your baskets with the ore and carried them back to the village, how do you separate the iron itself from the rock around it?

Bloom Furnace – Iron Ore

A bloom furnace is made in a similar way to the step kiln using a wooden frame covered with clay. The whole bloom furnace can stand between two and three feet high from the ground up and can measure between 1 and 2 feet wide. At the top of the furnace there is a wide hole and at the bottom where the furnace meets the ground you have a smaller hole. Below this smaller hole is a shallow channel of maybe 8 inches deep by 20 inches wide. This channel is used to collect the molten slag which will trickle out once the chemical reaction between the iron ore and the stone around it takes place at 800 degrees Centigrade. It is this chemical reaction which leaves us with an iron bloom ready for the blacksmith.

However, to get the temperature up to the critical 800 degrees, bellows are needed to pump oxygen into the furnace. Located about 1/3 of the up the furnace a small hole would have been left in the side so that the bellows could be inserted. To prepare the ore before adding to the furnace, you have to crush the rocks up until they resemble small gravel chips. You then mix this gravel with equal amounts of charcoal and place the mixture down into the furnace through the wide-open top.

Once the process has finished and the slag has trickles out into the channel at the bottom, the furnace must be left to cool down overnight. Once cooled, the iron blooms can be gathered together from inside the furnace.

They look a bit like dark grey pumice stone, and you can get a bloom about the size of a golf ball from three hand sized rocks. This shows just how labour intensive the industry was and how vital it was to the commerce and wealth of the tribe. On some sites, one can easily imagine that maybe up to three bloom furnaces were going at any one time.

Interestingly enough, whilst taking part in an Iron Age weekend in 2006 at the Cinderbury Iron Age site in Forest of Dean, England, I observed that the only way we could achieve the high enough temperature required, was when one of the 8 year old children involuntarily began operating the bellows with a rapid stamping action with his feet. Does this suggest that child labour was a normal feature of Iron Age life?

Iron Production 2 – Blacksmithing

Once the iron blooms were given to the Black Smith, then the hard work really began. All of the blooms would have been reheated in the Blacksmith's forge and then the smith and his apprentices would have spent the day continuously hammering out all of the impurities and carbon until the iron was good enough to make things out of. If he removed too much carbon, the iron became brittle and would break easily, if he left too much carbon in, then the iron would be too soft and would bend too easily.

What kinds of things did a Blacksmith make?

He made brooches, weapons and tools for the house and farm.

If the Blacksmith had too much iron, he would make it into currency bars like those found at Llyn Cerrig Bach on Anglesey and Castell Henllys in West Wales. We do not actually know how much one currency bar was worth, but we can guess. It doesn't take a lot to imagine that a currency bar resembles a spear head, a sickle or scythe blade or a sword and so, if only a noble or high status person could afford a sword, then perhaps this tells us that the currency bar was worth a lot of money.

So, imagine three industries. The blacksmith receiving the finished loom, the smelters producing the iron blooms and separating it out from the slag and then you have the charcoal burners who were very important because as we have seen, without them you wouldn't get the temperatures required to smelt the iron ore. This proves that the Celts were able to work together in an organized industry.

Fig. 32
An Iron Age Blacksmith at work.

Farming Techniques

Fig. 33

Experiments at Butser Ancient Farm in Hampshire, Southern England have proved that though the Gauls and Britons are usually remembered for being great warriors, they should perhaps be recognized as some of the best farmers Europe has ever seen.

The Iron Age people were so clever that in Britain it would be nearly 2000 years later before the same amount of land was under the plough.

What kind of crops did the Celts grow?
Barley, Wheat, Spelt, Flax and Hops as well as other crops which today we might class as weeds.

When springtime came and it was time to sow the seeds and plant their crops the Iron Age people used a basic plough called an Ard. The Ard is a wooden plough with a single handle and it would have been pulled by one or two Oxen or Dexter cattle. Unlike a modern plough, the Ard does not turn over a furrow; it simply scores a groove in the earth ready for the seeds.

Storage of seeds

By the time of the Iron Age, the hunter gatherer societies were as old to the Gauls and Britons as the Gauls and Britons are to us in the 21st Century. The Celts had mastered agriculture and farming. No longer were they dependent on finding natural seeds for their crops, in fact the Iron Age people had found an ingenious way of saving seeds through the winter months until sowing time the next spring.

On any established site, archaeologists find large numbers of pits in the ground. The Iron Age farmers stored their seeds in many of them over the winter. These pits were dug by hand, lined with clay, and allowed to dry. After the harvesting vast amounts of seed were poured into the pits almost to the brim, covered with leaves and then the pits were sealed with more clay.

Fig. 34
*Iron Age emmer
wheat.*

Inside, beneath the clay seal, only the top layer of seeds would begin to geminate until they had used up all the oxygen trapped in the pit. Then once all the oxygen had been used up most of the seeds were kept suspended in the vacuum until springtime when they were dug up, the top layer discarded, and the rest planted.

Harvesting

At harvest time, the whole community was involved gathering the crops in before the winter. Within living memory, in the early 20th Century echoes of what an Iron Age harvest may have looked like were still present. Teams of men with scythes worked clearing the fields probably accompanied by teams of women using small sickles to gather the crop into bundles or both working together making haystacks. The days were long hard toil necessary for the survival of the whole tribe. During the siege of Alesia in Gaul, Caesar tells us that the Romans were so successful on holding out against the surrounding Gaulish army that eventually the Gaul's had to leave the campaign to harvest their crops.

Without the safety nets that we enjoy in the 21st Century, if a crop failed in the Iron Age because of either too much rain, too little rain or pestilence then the tribe would have a very difficult winter and people were in very real danger of starvation and death.

The Granary

So, where did the communities store their sacks of ground flour and other perishable crops? The answer is, in a granary.

A granary is typically a small square building raised up on four stilt-like legs. The walls have small gaps between the planks allowing the air to circulate freely. This means there is less chance of the food rotting. But crops were not the only things to be kept in a granary, tallow or Beeswax candles could also be kept safe.

By keeping the granary off the ground on stilts makes it difficult for rats and other animals to get in and ruin the food.

There would have been quite a few granary structures in a village and in the countryside around. In fact, the same idea is used for the same purpose in countries like Spain and Austria today.

Fig. 35

Grinding Flour

Fig. 36
Saddle quern in use.

To grind flour, the Iron Age people, like the Romans used grinding stones which worked by having a stationary stone underneath and a second movable stone on top of it. Both stones were usually circular and were called Querns or more correctly, rotary Querns. The upper stone had a socket for one or two wooden handles (one on either side) and the operator would either turn the top stone continuously in a clockwise rotation or in the case of one handle, would simply move the top stone from side to side.

The un-milled wheat would be poured into the empty hole in the centre of the top stone. The milled flour spilt out of the tiny gap between the two stones and was collected ready for use. Another style is the earlier Saddle Quern which, instead of the upper stone rotating clockwise, a smaller stone is rubbed back and forth on the lower stone milling the wheat and oats into flour.

Fig. 37
Rotary quern in use.

Hearth & Home – The Clay Oven

The beehive shaped clay ovens inside most houses work on the same basis as a 19th Century wall oven would.

Fig. 38

At dawn, the central hearth would have its small fire rekindled and you would wait until the embers were red hot and glowing. With a small shovel, the hot embers are shoveled into the clay oven and the oven door is then closed to allow the air inside to heat up.

After about an hour, test the heat of the oven by placing your hand inside. The general rule of thumb is, if the small hairs on your wrist start to curl, then you know it is hot enough to bake.

- Rake out the remains of the embers.
- Place inside your flat breads or cake.
- Seal up the door again and wait until cooked.

The Iron Age people do not appear to have had yeast for bread and so their loaves may not have risen like modern loafs do. Their bread may have been an unleavened bread, made without yeast, similar in shape to pita style flat breads. Pita style flat breads only take about 5-10 minutes to bake in an Iron Age clay oven and were probably the last things to be made before people sat down for their meals.

Fig. 39

Fig. 40
With only naturally occurring yeast, few Iron Age loaves would have risen naturally.

Pottery Production – The Stepped Kiln

Pottery Kilns appear to have been made in the form of a step kiln. Most of the Iron Age people's pottery would have been made by hand. Once a pot is finished it would have been left outdoors to air dry until it had a leathery hardened finish.

Fig. 41

Updraught pottery kiln.

Before the stepped kiln, pots were placed in a bonfire and the fire lit. But the speed and temperature that the fire burnt at was difficult to control and sometimes, if the fire got too hot too quickly, the pottery would explode and break. So, the stepped kiln was a better way to fire pots.

The kilns are made, as the name suggests by cutting a step into a shallow bank of earth, maybe even the inner ramparts of a fort. Over this is placed a wicker work of sticks to create the basic shape. Then clay is added to cover the wooden wickerwork and once the clay has been left to dry out, a small fire can be lit in the bottom. This fire lit at the lower entrance burns away the wooden frame inside and hardens the clay interior ready for the controlled burns required for a successful kiln.

Inside, the pottery which you want to fire is placed on the shelf or step. Building a fire in the lower mouth of the kiln, you let it burn until the temperature inside is hot enough, and then you seal up both the entrances and leave it for 24 hours. This burns the oxygen in the kiln and in so doing, fires the pots.

Fig. 42

Fishing Techniques – Coracle Making

The coracle is a very lightweight boat which floats on top of the water like an acorn cup, so it is not hard to see where the Iron Age people got the idea from.

Due to its lightness and easy design, it was the perfect fishing boat for inland rivers and the fisherman could carry a coracle by himself supported on his back by a thick leather carry strap.

There are still skilled craftsmen in Wales and Ireland who build and use coracles today. They fish by stretching a net between two coracles side by side.

Old texts from Wales describe coracles and say that the best thing to cover them with is the hide of a bull. In fact, the size of the coracle is determined by the size of one bull hide.

So even after 2000 years, there have been almost no changes to the way a coracle is made. Most coracles are constructed using split ash or willow and sometimes hazel branches forming a lattice framework. The reinforced gunwale is also made from Ash. The Iron Age people would have grown willow for basket making and the shoots grow for three or four years to 9 to 10 feet and more than an inch in diameter— strong enough for building a coracle.

Before beginning to build a coracle, the Iron Age people would have known how important it is to ensure that the wood required had first been dried in the shade for at least six months and then soaked in water for a week prior to use. Using green or fresh material the framework will later shrink and not create the tight construction the boat requires.

This proves that forethought and planning were important, and no self-respecting Gaul or Briton would ever decide simply on the spur of the moment to attempt to make one.

Fig. 43

How to build you own Coracle

In some places the coracle is still used today, if you wanted to try making your own, here is how:

- With a piece of string lay out an extended oval measuring 3 1/2 feet wide by 4 1/2 feet long.
- Then with an iron bar make holes around the inside edge of the string every 8 inches for the 32 ribs.
- Now push in the sharpened ends of each willow or hazel rib. Make sure they lean outward at a slight angle, into the holes.
- Next, select willow or hazel sticks which must be no thicker than 1/2 inch at their widest
- Then create the gunwale, lay a stick behind each rib, and begin to weave these 32 strands around the ribs in a one- over, one-under pattern, just like wattling a fence or hurdle. Keep doing it until it measures about 6 inches high.
- Now the ribs must be bent over so the coracle will take on its final shape. Ensure that the opposing ends of the willow or hazel ribs are placed into the ground on the opposite side of the craft. The side to side ribs are bent first, with the front and back ribs laid on top of them for strength.
- Once done, using tarred twine, lash all the crosspieces in a crisscross fashion firmly together.

At this stage, the frame can be pulled from the ground ready for the waterproofed covering to be sewn in place. You may find it easier to balance the wickerwork frame on your workshop tabletop. Now originally, this is when the Iron Age craftsmen would have visited their tanner to obtain a bull hide. Modern coracle makers use a heavy weight No. 10 sail maker's canvas instead.

- Stretch the canvas over the frame and sew in place temporarily.
- Next trim off any excess material and roll the edges up to the gun-

wale. After adjusting it to get the canvas folds evenly spaced, stitch the canvas to the gunwale using waxed linen thread, triangle-shaped sail maker's needles and sail maker's sewing palm.

- It is especially important to ensure that the canvas is pulled tight. Once the canvas is sewed on, it is time to paint a waterproofing mixture. Apply a thick coating of the mixture: with a piece of spare canvas, rub the sealant deeply into the canvas. Let this dry overnight and repeat the process again the next day. Then give the coracle two coats of oil-based deck paint.

Waterproofing

Originally, the hide covering was made waterproof by tarring or pitching. To make 1 gallon of waterproofing combine the following ingredients this can be obtained at art supply or paint stores.

43 ounces boiled linseed oil,

21 ounces paint thinner,

34 ounces porch and deck enamel,

2 ounces drier,

6 1/2 pounds silica (obtained from a pottery)

2 ounces spar varnish.

Where do I sit?

The final step is to make a seat. The seat in a coracle runs side to side and is supported in the middle by a 2-foot-by-2-inch square piece of spruce, notched to fit the ribs and held to the seat with a couple of dowels glued in place. The seat can generally expect to measure, 8 inches by 1 inch by 3 1/2 feet.

Coracles are paddled, or more correctly sculled, not to the stern but rather toward the prow using a figure-eight stroke. If you start paddling to the side, like you might in a canoe, you will simply spend the day going round and round in circles.

Tools

Tools that the Iron Age people required: Hammer, Pliers, Anvil, Small Saw, Spoke-shave, Hot iron nail for burning holes through wood, Wooden dowel, Wood Glue, Sharp Knife, Bone needle and strong thread.

*** If you have never made or used a coracle before we strongly recommend that you contact: The Coracle Society. Their contact information can be found in the acknowledgements section at the back of this book.

Be smart, wear a life jacket!!

Tallow Candles

Tallow candles are made by melting beef fat very slowly over five days. The fat needs to melt so slowly that it looks like it is only sweating. By melting the tallow so slowly, you eventually get liquid tallow.

Before cooling, sieve off any big lumps and gristle. If the fat was melted at the right temperature, the end product will be an off white colour. If it is a dull shade of brown, then it got too hot and burnt. But either way, the result is candle making material.

Before dipping candle wicks into the cooling tallow, you should mix a small amount of beeswax into the mixture. This gives you hardened candles, rather than soft ones which burn too quickly.

Making these candles is not labour intensive; however, it does take patience to sit and dip the wicks repeatedly. If tallow candles were used regularly then perhaps the Iron Age people would have made them during the summer months ready for the winter months. The candles once lit and depending on their thickness will burn anywhere from ½ hour to 1 hour each.

Storing tallow candles was important too because tallow can attract mice and in later centuries, the candles were always stored in metal boxes. How did the Iron Age communities store theirs?

Tallow candles were not the only light source available, in an Iron Age village there were a variety of light sources, tallow candles, beeswax candles, fish oil lamps with a floating wick and in the higher status houses maybe even pottery oil lamps from the Classical world.

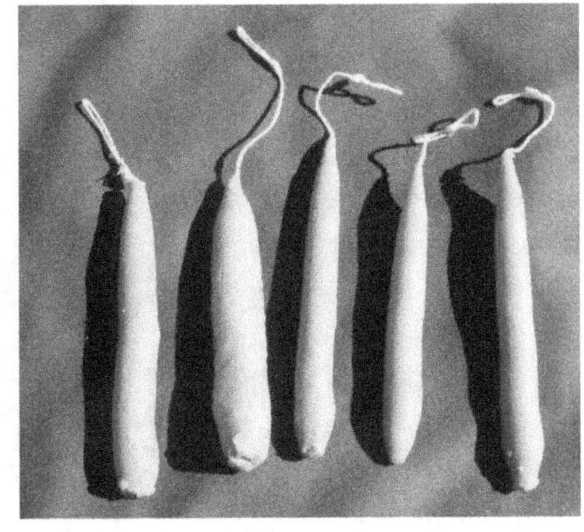

Fig. 44

Iron Age Soap

Did you know that soap is almost certainly an invention attributed to the Britons and Gauls? So, remember, next time you are in the bath, the Romans may have invented baths, but it was the Britons and Gauls whom invented the soap!

Iron Age soap would have been made using a mixture of water, lye, lanolin, and various animal fats. The Britons & Gauls would have used wooden bowls or vats, or maybe even barrels for soap production. If they had had aluminium they would have noticed that Lye will burn right through it! If you are thinking about trying to make your own Iron Age soap, you need know a little bit about lye**.

It is perhaps better known as sodium hydroxide. Fats for soap making include animal fats such as tallow & lard. In the Iron Age, animal fats were used, with beef tallow making the hardest soap, pork lard a medium hardness soap and hen fat the softest. It is generally accepted that the harder fats make better soap.

Making soap does not happen all at once but takes days to complete and then 2-6 weeks to dry out or cure depending on the fat used.

Once mixed and having waited for the necessary chemical reactions to take place between the ingredients, the Iron Age people would have used a wooden box in the shape of a tray with a cloth laid in the bottom of it. The cloth was used to help remove the hardened soap from the tray. When the

Fig. 45

"

soap begins to harden (1 hour to 3 days depending on how fast the curing process is moving along) the makers would section it into bars using a knife. Even though the soap looks hard at this stage, it is far from done. There is a good chance it contains a bit of lye that should be left to complete its chemical reaction. With the soap out of the tray, the Iron Age people would have stacked it up and set it in a warm dry place for at least two weeks. When it fully cured, they would place it in a bag or airtight container, and store it in a cool, dry place maybe even in a granary like building.

What are the best fats for soap making? Well, it seems that lard beats tallow and vegetable oils for gentleness to your skin. However, you may be surprised. In an age when modern soap makers tell us that soap needs lots of bubbles to work, Iron Age soap made with 100% lard does not lather very well. But it cleans splendidly!

** If you get Lye on you, you will find it is very bad stuff. Never allow children or pets anywhere near it!! Also be careful what kind of mixing utensils and mixing containers you use during production. If you insist on trying to make Iron Age soap, you must wear eye protection and rubber gloves when handling the lye solution after you have mixed it into the water.

The Art of Dry-Stone Walling

Have you ever stood outside a field that is surrounded by a dry-stone wall and been confused because you cannot find the gate?

Even today in parts of Ireland, the farmer will simply take down a section of the wall to allow his cows or sheep to walk in, and then he will rebuild the wall behind them.

Dry stone walling is perhaps one of the earliest skills developed by ancient man. Even 3000 years before the Gauls and Britons, the people who lived in the village of Skara Brae, on Orkney, were able to build houses and furniture with the technique.

Fig. 46

All over Europe, enormous Iron Age fortified communities were defended by what the Romans called 'Murus Gallicus' or 'The Gaulish Wall". The walls were by this time constructed around timber frames. Tight stone walling with no mortar between them faced the inside and outside whilst rubble and hard packed earth filled the centre.

Dry stone walling lasts so long because there is no mortar to crack and crumble away. It is held in lace only by the weight of the combined stones and by the skillful eye of the builder who first selected and placed the stones on top of one another.

However, In Britain the Iron Age farmers did not build chest high walls between fields. For the most part they simply seem to have marked out the edges of their fields with stones stacked loosely up to about ankle height. Preferring Dry Stone walling for Defence & Roundhouse construction.

Woodland Management & Coppicing

If you have ever been lucky enough to spend time in an Iron Age village re-construction, you will appreciate that if the Iron Age people had no knowledge of woodland management and coppicing, then a small community of 100 people would have stripped the landscape around them bare within a generation. Permanent Iron Age settlements would have been incapable of supporting life on a continuous basis.

Archaeological excavations prove that communities continued for many generations proves undoubtedly that as well as being remarkably successful farmers, the Gauls and Britons understood sustainable woodland management even if that title is a modern term.

Coppicing is the knowledge that by cutting trees to ground level allows vigorous re-growth and a continuous supply of specific timber for future tribal community requirements. For instance, Hazel and willow was a mainstay of the construction industry well into medieval times and the Iron Age people knew that it takes a 7-year growth cycle before the willow and hazel is ready for coracle building as well as house construction. Good woodland management allows coppiced trees to live longer than un-coppiced trees would live if they had been left untouched. This is because coppicing allows lots of sunlight back onto the forest floor and the more sun the greater the growth.

The Gentle Art of Basketmaking

Basket making is an incredibly old art and was ancient even to the Iron Age people.

Fig. 47

The best material for basket making is willow and hazel. When made well, the finished results are strong, rigid, and reliable, but most importantly are light weight.

It is difficult to say whether each community had its own basket weavers or whether everyone simply made their own when needed.

These early baskets would have been known as frame baskets and could be constructed quite easily if you have a spare afternoon. They are easy to make but time consuming.

What were baskets used for? Well take a look around your house. Every cardboard box you have would have been a basket. Every small rubbish bin would have been a basket. What else could you think a basket might be used for?

If you were a gardener, you would have used a basket to collect your vegetables in. Sheep's wool could be kept in baskets, fish, poultry even eggs could all be stored in baskets of different shapes and sizes with or what else can you use basket making skills to construct? Well, it may surprise you, but you can make great fish traps, bird cages and even crab catchers without lids.!

Fig. 48

An example of a fish trap.

Flint Knapping

Flint Knapping is another process which was as old to the Iron Age people as they are to us today, in fact even older! Almost 3 million years to be exact!

Before a razor edge could be created with copper, bronze or Iron, the only way to create such a razor-sharp edge was to knap a distinctive looking rock named flint. Knapping is the name given to the craft of making edged tools i.e. arrowheads & drill points not to mention scrapers for tanning and curing leather from flint.

Flint knapping is basically a reduction process because flakes of stone are broken off the original piece of stone. Flint knappers like to joke that in order to make an arrowhead, you simply knap off all the bits that do not look like an arrowhead, until you are left with, the arrowhead.

Fig. 49

How to Flint Knapp

Before you do anything, find a comfortable place to sit with plenty of daylight. Next ensure you have a pair of safety goggles and a sheepskin. The sheepskin should be placed over your legs because the flint is so sharp, that without it, you could easily cut yourself.

Generally, you begin knapping a piece of stone with direct percussion. Meaning, you strike the edge of the flint with a larger harder material, sometimes a stone, sometimes a piece of deer antler. Starting this way helps you remove the larger pieces of flint.

The next step is to use a smaller pointed tool, such as antler or granite as a pressure flaker. Use this on the edge of the flint and apply an inward pressure to the tool. This pressure will remove a small, thin flake from the edge of the flint. Pressure flaking shapes and refines the projectile point and the fluted neck of an arrowhead.

Flint Knapping is not as easy as it looks, and it takes practice and an experienced eye to know where the best place to strike the flint is. If you get it wrong, you will break the arrowhead that has just taken you an hour to almost finish.

It is interesting to note that until the invention of the razor blade; only one other tool was considered sharper than flint. The black stone Obsidian is so sharp it used to be used for eye surgery within living memory.

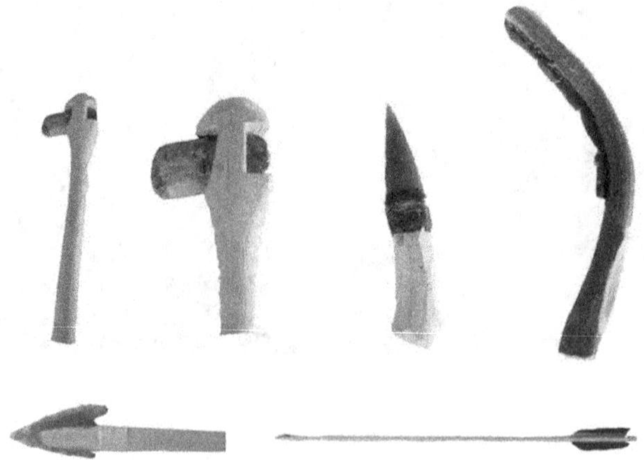

Fig. 50

The Gentle Art of Wood Turning

Even today, thanks to the Romans, many people still believe the Iron Age people were technologically challenged.

But far from having to make do with roughhewn wooden objects, we know that the Britons and Gauls were able to create spokes and axles for their chariots, bowls, plates, spear shafts and door fittings using pole lathes.

The pole lathe is made from timber and it allows a craftsman to turn wood accurately. The pole lathe, though an ancient tool, is still popular today. This is because it is simple to make from a coppice pole and a few other pieces of wood.

When the craftsman has a piece of wood to be worked, he would place it in between two fixed points on the lathe itself. The piece to be carved is then rotated by what might have been a leather cord that passes around it.

This leather cord is fixed by one end to a foot pedal, and at the other to a flexible sapling. As the foot peddle is pushed down, the cord rotates the piece of wood to make the cutting stroke, at the same time bending the sapling. As the peddle is released, the sapling straightens, rotating the piece of wood away to make the return, non-cutting stroke.

Unlike modern electric operated lathes, the pole lathe is safe to operate. This is because the piece of wood that is being carved will stop turning the moment the foot peddle is stopped. The speed can be adjusted by the speed at which the craftsman presses the foot peddle.

We can imagine seeing pole lathes set up in the woodland or in an Iron Age village. The other good thing about using a pole lathe is that when turning green wood, there is no dust or splinters.

These pole lathes cannot have been poorly constructed tools put together with little forethought, a good pole lathe takes time and effort to build and of course the result is all about quality.

The Iron Age craftsmen would have chosen hardwood for preference or denser grained softwood. Good woods would be Oak, ash, and beech because when in use, the lathe takes a lot of punishment and so resilience is especially important.

Fig. 51 (left)
Turned bowls & plates.

Fig. 52 (right)
A Sapling Pole Lathe

Conclusion

At many Iron Age archaeological sites, we find evidence for outside or community hearths. Until the arrival of the Roman's we have little evidence to suggest that the Gauls and Britons had buildings specifically to use as pubs or 'taverna's' as the Roman's called them. But just like in the 21st Century people would naturally have wanted to get together after their day or week of work and toil. They would perhaps have eaten together, told stories, jokes and maybe even sung together. They no doubt probably even got drunk together.

So for the Britons and Gauls, far from being a barbaric people who, as the Romans have had us believe for the last 2000 years were incapable of nothing more than eating mud, wearing mud and living in mud huts just waiting for the Roman's to bring us the light of civilization, we can see that Iron Age societies in Britain and Europe were a very complex thinking, problem solving, hardworking and in many respects a well-organized society.

Acknowledgements

Amgueddfa Cymru - National Museum Wales
Butser Ancient Farm
Brigantia Iron Age Re-enactment Group
David Freeman – Gallica
Pembrokeshire Coast National Park
Ron & Brenda Phillips – Surviving the Iron Age
National Geographic Magazine
Novium Museum

Useful Contacts:

The Coracle Society: 3 Back Lane Wereham King's Lynn
Norfolk PE33 9BB
United Kingdom

Image Credits:

Courtesy of Bodrifty Farm UK
    Fig. 21
Courtesy of Butser Ancient Farm
    Fig. 17, 19, 33, 34, 38
Courtesy of Canterbury Archaeological Society
    Fig. 42
Courtesy of Canterbury Trust
    Fig. 40
Courtesy of Castell Henllys Iron Age Fort, Pembrokeshire National Park
    Fig. 35
Courtesy of The Coracle Society
    Fig. 43
Courtesy of Historic England
    Fig. 50

Courtesy of Llawerch Productions

Fig. 3-16, 18, 24-32, 39, 41, 44-49, 51-52

Courtesy of National Geographic

Fig. 1-2

Courtesy of Pembrokeshire National Park

Fig. 22-23, 36-37

Courtesy of St Fagans Museum

Fig. 20